· Cooking for Today ·

CLASSIC HOME COOKING

·*Cooking for Today*·

CLASSIC HOME COOKING

ROSEMARY WADEY

|| ·**PARRAGON**· ||

First published in Great Britain in 1996 by
Parragon Book Service Ltd
Unit 13-17, Avonbridge Trading Estate
Atlantic Road
Avonmouth
Bristol BS11 9QD

ISBN 0-7525-1803-8

Produced by Haldane Mason, London

Printed in Italy

Acknowledgements:
Art Direction: Ron Samuels
Editor: Vicky Hanson
Series Design: Pedro & Frances Prá-Lopez/Kingfisher Design, London
Page Design: Somewhere Creative
Photography: Joff Lee
Styling: John Lee Studios
Home Economist: Rosemary Wadey

Photographs on pages 6, 20, 34, 48, 62 reproduced by permission of
ZEFA Picture Library (UK) Ltd

Note:
Cup measurements in this book are for American cups. Tablespoons are assumed to be 15 ml.
Unless otherwise stated, milk is assumed to be full-fat, eggs are standard size 2
and pepper is freshly ground black pepper.

Contents

CHAPTER ONE

Soups & Starters

A traditional dinner is often a three-course affair, beginning with something to whet the appetite and set the tone for the rest of the meal. Consequently, the first course has to be carefully selected so that it complements the following courses and does not overwhelm them or overfill your guests.

Whether you serve a soup or another type of appetizer depends greatly on the rest of the menu. It is best not to serve a thick, meaty soup before a rich casserole or stew, but it could be ideal before a light or cold dish and, served with crusty bread and a selection of cheeses, thick soups make excellent lunch or supper dishes. Also bear in mind the weather when deciding your menu; on a hot summer's day your guests may be surprised if served a thick, hearty soup.

Many appetizers can also be served as a snack or light meal. Marinated Country Mushrooms, in a simple tarragon dressing, are so quick to prepare and can be left to marinate for anything from 30 minutes to two hours. Potted Meat can be quickly and simply made from leftover cooked meats or poultry and is quite on a par with the tastiest of pâtés. To turn your starter into something special, packets of mixed salad leaves are a convenient way to add colour and freshness and they're ideal as a base or garnish.

Opposite: Fresh vegetables made into a soup or salad are perfect for a light starter that won't ruin your guests' appetites.

STEP 1

STEP 1

STEP 4

STEP 5

THICK ONION SOUP

A delicious creamy soup with grated carrot and parsley for texture and colour. Serve with crusty cheese scones for a hearty starter or lunch.

SERVES 4–6

75 g/ 2½ oz/ 5 tbsp butter or margarine
500 g/ 1 lb onions, chopped finely
1 garlic clove, crushed
45 g/ 1½ oz/ 6 tbsp plain (all-purpose) flour
600 ml/ 1 pint/ 2½ cups chicken or
  vegetable stock
600 ml/ 1 pint/ 2½ cups milk
2–3 tsp lemon or lime juice
good pinch of ground allspice
1 bay leaf
1 carrot, grated coarsely
4–6 tbsp double (heavy) cream (optional)
2 tbsp chopped fresh parsley
salt and pepper

CHEESE SCONES:
250 g/ 8 oz/ 2 cups malted wheat or
  wholemeal (whole wheat) flour
2 tsp baking powder
60 g/ 2 oz/ ¼ cup butter or margarine
4 tbsp grated Parmesan cheese
1 egg, beaten
about 75 ml/ 3 fl oz/ ⅓ cup milk

1 Melt the butter or margarine in a saucepan and fry the onions and garlic gently for 10–15 minutes, stirring frequently, until soft but not coloured. Stir in the flour and cook for a minute or so, then gradually stir in the stock and bring to the boil, stirring frequently. Add the milk, then bring back to the boil.

2 Add the seasoning, 2 teaspoons of lemon or lime juice, the allspice and bay leaf. Cover and simmer for about 25 minutes until the vegetables are tender. Discard the bay leaf.

3 Meanwhile, make the scones. Combine the flour, baking powder and seasoning and rub in the butter or margarine until the mixture resembles fine breadcrumbs. Stir in 3 tablespoons of the cheese, then add the egg and enough milk to mix to a soft dough.

4 Shape into a bar about 2 cm/ ¾ inch thick. Place on a floured baking sheet (cookie sheet) and mark into slices. Sprinkle with the remaining cheese and bake in a preheated oven at 220°C/425°F/Gas Mark 7 for about 20 minutes until risen and golden brown.

5 Stir the carrot into the soup and simmer for 2–3 minutes. Adjust the seasoning and add more lemon or lime juice, if necessary. Stir in the cream, if using, and reheat gently. Sprinkle with the parsley and serve with the warm scones, broken into fingers.

ASPARAGUS SOUP

*Fresh asparagus is now available for most of the year, so this soup can
be made at any time. It can also be made using canned asparagus.*

STEP 1

STEP 3

STEP 5

STEP 6

SERVES 4–6

*1 bunch asparagus, about 350 g/12 oz,
    or 2 packs mini asparagus, about 150 g/
    5 oz each*
*700 ml/1¼ pints/3 cups chicken or
    vegetable stock*
60 g/2 oz/¼ cup butter or margarine
1 onion, chopped
3 tbsp plain (all-purpose) flour
¼ tsp ground coriander
1 tbsp lemon juice
450 ml/¾ pint/2 cups milk
*4–6 tbsp double (heavy) or single (light)
    cream or fromage frais*
salt and pepper

1 Wash and trim the asparagus,
discarding the woody part of the
stem. Cut the remainder into short
lengths, keeping a few tips for garnish.
Mini asparagus does not need to be
trimmed.

2 Cook the tips in the minimum of
boiling salted water for 5–10
minutes. Drain and set aside.

3 Put the asparagus in a saucepan
with the stock, bring to the boil,
cover and simmer for about 20 minutes
until soft. Drain and reserve the stock.

4 Melt the butter or margarine in a
saucepan and fry the onion very
gently until soft, but only barely
coloured. Stir in the flour and cook for a
minute or so then stir in the reserved
stock and bring to the boil.

5 Simmer the sauce for 2–3 minutes
until thickened, then stir in the
cooked asparagus, seasoning, coriander
and lemon juice. Simmer for 10 minutes,
then cool a little and either press through
a sieve (strainer), or mix in a blender or
food processor until smooth.

6 Pour into a clean pan, add the milk
and reserved asparagus tips and
bring to the boil. Adjust the seasoning
and simmer for 2 minutes. Stir in the
cream or fromage frais and reheat gently.

CANNED
ASPARAGUS

If using canned asparagus, drain off the
liquid and use as part of the measured
stock. Remove a few small asparagus tips
for garnish and chop the remainder.
Continue as above.

OXTAIL SOUP

A real old-fashioned, meaty soup with plenty of flavour from the added vegetables, herbs and wine; almost a meal in itself.

STEP 1

STEP 2

STEP 3

STEP 5

SERVES 6

1 oxtail
2 tbsp vegetable oil
2 onions, sliced
2 carrots, sliced
2 celery sticks, sliced
2 litres/ 3¹/₂ pints/ 2 quarts brown or beef
   stock
2 slices bacon, derinded and chopped
1 fresh bouquet garni
45 g/ 1¹/₂ oz/ 3 tbsp butter or margarine
45 g/ 1¹/₂ oz/ 6 tbsp plain (all-purpose) flour
1 tbsp lemon juice
3–4 tbsp port (optional)
2 tbsp chopped fresh parsley
salt and pepper
fresh crusty bread to serve

1 Cut the oxtail into slices about 5 cm/2 inches thick, or ask the butcher to do it for you. Trim the excess fat from the oxtail.

2 Heat the oil in a large saucepan and fry the oxtail until beginning to brown. Add the vegetables and fry for about 5 minutes until well browned. Pour any excess fat from the pan.

3 Add the stock, bacon and bouquet garni and bring to the boil. Skim off any scum from the surface, cover the pan and simmer very gently for 3–4 hours until the meat is very tender. As oxtail is very fatty, it is necessary to skim the soup occasionally during cooking to remove as much fat from the surface as possible.

4 Strain the soup and, if time allows, cool and chill so a layer of fat solidifies on the surface and can easily be lifted off. Alternatively, skim off excess fat from the surface with kitchen paper.

5 Remove the meat from the bones and chop it neatly. If liked, purée the vegetables in a food processor or blender or pass through a sieve (strainer) and place in a clean pan with the strained soup and chopped meat. Alternatively, leave the vegetables whole. Reheat gently.

6 Blend the butter or margarine and flour and gradually whisk small pieces into the soup. Simmer until thickened.

7 Add the lemon juice, then the port, if using. Adjust the seasoning and reheat gently. Sprinkle with parsley and serve piping hot with fresh crusty bread.

MARINATED COUNTRY MUSHROOMS

Marinated button mushrooms with a hint of tarragon can be served with a mixed leaf salad and croûtons for a delicious appetizer.

STEP 1

SERVES 4

500 g/ 1 lb button mushrooms
4 tbsp olive oil
4 tbsp sunflower oil
2 garlic cloves, crushed
1 tbsp wholegrain mustard
good pinch of sugar
2 tbsp white wine vinegar
1 tbsp chopped fresh tarragon or 1 tsp dried
    tarragon
2–3 tbsp soured cream
salt and pepper

CROUTONS:
3 slices white bread
about 4 tbsp olive oil
1 garlic clove, crushed

TO SERVE:
mixed salad leaves
crisply fried bacon, crumbled (optional)

1 Trim the mushrooms, cutting the stems off level with the caps. Wipe the mushrooms and place in a large bowl. If the mushrooms are large, halve or quarter them.

2 Whisk together the olive and sunflower oils, garlic, mustard, sugar, seasoning and vinegar until

completely emulsified, then add the tarragon.

STEP 3

3 Pour the dressing over the mushrooms, toss them thoroughly in the dressing and leave to marinate for at least 30 minutes and up to 2 hours, giving an occasional stir so they are all well coated.

4 To make the croûtons, remove the crusts from the bread and cut it into 1 cm/½ inch cubes. Heat the oil with the garlic in a frying pan (skillet) and fry the bread cubes for a few minutes until golden brown. Drain thoroughly on paper towels.

STEP 5

5 Drain the mushrooms, reserving the marinade. Mix 3 tablespoons of the marinade with the soured cream and season to taste.

6 Arrange the salad leaves on individual serving plates and spoon the mushrooms on top. Spoon the dressing over the mushrooms, then sprinkle with the croûtons and bacon, if using, and serve.

STEP 6

STEP 1

STEP 2

STEP 5

STEP 6

SALMON MOUSSE

This mousse looks very impressive if served in a fish-shaped mould, but it will taste just as good if it is set in a plain dish or individual dishes. Decorate the top with cucumber and olives.

SERVES 6–8

30 g/1 oz/2 tbsp butter or margarine
30 g/1 oz/4 tbsp plain (all-purpose) flour
300 ml/¹/₂ pint/1¹/₄ cups milk
¹/₂ tsp mustard
good pinch of chilli powder
2 tbsp white wine vinegar
2 eggs, separated
300–350 g/10–12 oz cooked salmon
150 ml/¹/₄ pint/²/₃ cup double (heavy) or
 soured cream
4 tsp powdered gelatine
3 tbsp water
salt and pepper
Melba Toast (see page 76) to serve

TO GARNISH:
basil sprigs
stuffed green olives or black olives
cucumber slices
salad leaves

1 Melt the butter or margarine in a saucepan, stir in the flour and cook for a minute or so. Gradually stir in the milk and bring to the boil. Add the mustard, chilli powder, seasoning and vinegar and simmer for 2 minutes. Beat in the egg yolks and simmer for 1 minute, stirring constantly, then remove from the heat.

2 Flake the salmon, discarding any skin and bones, and stir into the sauce.

3 Lightly whip the double (heavy) cream, if using, until thick but not too stiff and fold this or the soured cream into the sauce.

4 Dissolve the gelatine in the water in a small bowl over a saucepan of hot water, or in a microwave oven set on Medium power. Cool slightly then stir evenly through the salmon mixture. Leave until on the point of setting.

5 Beat the egg whites until stiff then fold into the salmon mixture. Pour into an oiled fish mould, a serving dish or individual dishes. Chill until set.

6 If using a dish or individual dishes, garnish the top with slices of olive and cucumber. If the mousse has been set in a mould, loosen it from the mould and turn out carefully on to a flat dish. Garnish with basil sprigs, olives, slices of cucumber and salad leaves and serve.

STEP 1

STEP 3

STEP 4

STEP 5

POTTED MEAT

Cooked meats, poultry and game can all be prepared in this traditional way: finely minced (ground) and cooked with onions, spices and sherry or port. Serve as a first course or sandwich filling.

SERVES 4–6

250 g/8 oz cooked beef, lamb or any
*   boneless game or poultry*
125 g/4 oz/½ cup butter
1 onion, chopped very finely or minced
1–2 garlic cloves, crushed
2 tbsp sherry or port
about 4 tbsp good stock
good pinch of ground mace, nutmeg or
*   allspice*
pinch of dried mixed herbs
salt and pepper
sprigs of fresh thyme to garnish

TO SERVE:
watercress sprigs
cherry tomatoes or tomato slices or wedges
fingers of toast or crusty bread

1 Remove any skin, gristle and bone from the meat, game or poultry and then finely mince (grind) twice, or finely chop in a food processor.

2 Melt half the butter in a saucepan and fry the onion and garlic gently until soft but only lightly coloured.

3 Stir the meat into the pan, followed by the sherry or port and just enough stock to moisten.

4 Season to taste with salt, pepper, mace and herbs. Press the mixture into a lightly greased dish or several small individual dishes and level the top. Chill until firm.

5 Melt the remaining butter and pour a thin layer over the potted meat. Add a few sprigs of fresh herbs and chill thoroughly so the herbs set in the butter.

6 Serve the potted meat spooned on to plates, or in individual pots on plates, garnished with watercress, tomatoes and fingers of toast or crusty bread.

STORAGE

The potted meat will keep in the refrigerator for 2–3 days but no longer, as it does not contain any preservatives.
  If you wish to keep it longer, it can be frozen for up to 1 month.

CHAPTER TWO

Fish

Fish is easy to prepare (indeed, it can usually be bought ready-prepared) and quick to cook and is a healthy option for a wide range of tastes and ages, including semi-vegetarians – it is low in calories and fat and provides protein, vitamins and minerals.

Fish dishes are extremely versatile – Ocean Pie, containing a variety of fish and prawns (shrimp), makes a good everyday meal but can also be dressed up with whole prawns (shrimp) and an attractive garnish and served for an elegant meal. Also suitable for a special occasion is a whole salmon, gently poached, cooled, skinned and glazed in aspic for an impressive main course or part of a buffet spread.

Whenever you serve fish, the main point to remember is that it must always be very fresh – try to cook it within 24 hours, and always store it in the refrigerator. Bought frozen fish is excellent, but must be used very quickly after thawing. If you intend to freeze fish yourself, always check that it has not been previously frozen and thawed.

Opposite: *Make sure the fish you buy is fresh – it should have firm flesh, bright eyes and should not have a strong smell.*

STEP 1

STEP 2

STEP 2

STEP 5

HERRINGS IN OATMEAL

Fillets of herring do away with the problem of bones, and here they are coated in oatmeal, fried or baked and serve with a hollandaise sauce flavoured with herbs, mustard and orange rind.

SERVES 4

4 herrings, about 350 g/12 oz each, cleaned
1 egg, beaten
about 125 g/4 oz/1 cup fine or medium
    oatmeal or 150 g/5 oz/1¼ cups coarse
    oatmeal
60 g/2 oz/¼ cup butter or margarine
    (optional)
2 tbsp oil
salt and pepper

MUSTARD HOLLANDAISE SAUCE:
2 tbsp tarragon vinegar
1 tbsp water
2 egg yolks, lightly beaten
90–125 g/3–4 oz/⅓–½ cup butter, diced
    and softened slightly
1 tbsp chopped fresh mixed herbs
1 tbsp wholegrain mustard
grated rind of ½ small orange

TO GARNISH:
orange slices
fresh herbs

1 Cut the heads off the herrings then open out, flesh side down, on a flat surface. Press very firmly along the backbone of the fish with your thumbs or the heel of your hand; this loosens the backbone.

2 Turn the fish over and carefully ease out the backbone and any other loose bones. Cut each fish lengthways into 2 fillets, rinse in cold water and dry thoroughly. Season lightly, then dip in beaten egg and coat in oatmeal, pressing it on well. Set aside.

3 To make the sauce, put the vinegar and water into a saucepan and boil until reduced by half. Put the egg yolks into a bowl and stir in the vinegar. Stand the bowl over a pan of simmering water and heat gently, stirring, until the mixture thickens. (Don't let the water boil or the sauce will curdle.)

4 Whisk in the butter, a little at a time. Stir in the herbs, mustard, orange rind and seasoning.

5 Melt the butter and oil in a frying pan (skillet) and fry the fish for 4–5 minutes on each side until golden brown. Alternatively, place the fish in a greased baking tin (pan), drizzle over a little oil and cook in a preheated oven at 180°C/ 350°F/Gas Mark 4 for about 30 minutes.

6 Garnish with orange slices and herbs and serve with the mustard hollandaise sauce.

STEP 2

STEP 4

STEP 5

STEP 6

GLAZED SALMON

*This is one of the traditional ways of serving a whole cold salmon.
Glaze it with aspic and spend a little time on an attractive garnish to
make a splendid centrepiece for a buffet table.*

SERVES 8–12

*2–3 kg/4–6 lb whole salmon, cleaned, with
    head left on
3–4 bay leaves
300 ml/¹/₂ pint/1¹/₄ cups white wine vinegar
1¹/₂ tsp black peppercorns
4 cloves
1–2 onions, sliced thinly
1 lemon, sliced thinly*

*TO GARNISH:
about 450 ml/³/₄ pint/2 cups liquid aspic
    jelly
cucumber slices
stuffed green olives
mixed salad leaves
cherry tomatoes or tomato wedges
lime or lemon slices or wedges*

1 Wipe the fish inside and out and, if
liked, put 2 bay leaves in the cavity.
Half fill a fish kettle with water. Add the
vinegar, bay leaves, peppercorns and
cloves and bring slowly to the boil.

2 Lay the salmon on the metal rack
with the onions and lemon slices
and carefully lower it into the fish kettle.

3 Bring slowly back to the boil, cover
and then simmer very gently – the

water must not boil – allowing 5 minutes
per 500 g/1 lb.

4 Remove the kettle from the heat
and leave the fish to cool in the
water in a cold place. When quite cold,
remove the fish carefully, drain and chill.
Carefully strip the skin off the fish.

5 Make up the aspic jelly following
the directions on the packet. Leave
to cool, then chill half of it. When it
begins to thicken, brush a layer over the
whole fish, including the head. Add a
second and possibly a third layer of aspic
to give an even coating.

6 When set, transfer the fish to a
serving dish. Garnish with thin
slices of cucumber and sliced stuffed
olives dipped in aspic so that they stick.
Add a final layer of aspic jelly to the
whole fish and chill until set. Garnish
with salad leaves, tomatoes and lime or
lemon slices or twists.

SOUSED TROUT

Fillets of trout are gently poached in a spiced vinegar, left to marinate for 24 hours and served cold with potato salad

STEP 1

SERVES 4

4 trout, about 250–350 g/8–12 oz each,
  filleted
1 onion, sliced very thinly
2 bay leaves, preferably fresh
sprigs of fresh parsley and dill or other fresh
  herbs
10–12 black peppercorns
4–6 cloves
good pinch of salt
150 ml/¼ pint/⅔ cup red wine vinegar
salad leaves to garnish

POTATO SALAD:
500 g/1 lb small new potatoes
2 tbsp French dressing
4 tbsp thick mayonnaise
3–4 spring onions (scallions), sliced

1 Trim the trout fillets, cutting off any pieces of fin. If preferred, remove the skin – use a sharp knife and, beginning at the tail end, carefully cut the flesh from the skin, pressing the knife down firmly as you go.

2 Lightly grease a shallow ovenproof dish and lay the fillets in it, packing them fairly tightly together but keeping in a single layer. Arrange the sliced onion, bay leaves and herbs over the fish.

3 Put the peppercorns, cloves, salt and vinegar into a saucepan and bring almost to the boil. Remove from the heat and pour evenly over the fish.

4 Cover with foil and cook in a preheated oven at 160°C/325°F/ Gas Mark 3 for 15 minutes. Leave until cold and then chill thoroughly.

5 Meanwhile, make the potato salad. Cook the potatoes in boiling salted water for 10–15 minutes until just tender. Drain. While still warm, cut into large dice and place in a bowl. Combine the French dressing and mayonnaise, add to the potatoes while warm and toss evenly. Leave until cold, then sprinkle with chopped spring onions (scallions).

6 Serve each portion of fish with a little of the juices, garnished with salad leaves and accompanied by the potato salad.

STEP 2

STEP 3

VARIATION

Fillets of herring can be cooked in the same way.

STEP 5

27

STEP 1

STEP 3

STEP 4

STEP 5

SKATE WITH BLACK BUTTER

Skate wings look bony but the flesh, which has a pale pink tinge, is easily picked off the bones when the fish is cooked. A piquant caper and butter sauce is a perfect accompaniment.

SERVES 4

4 skate wings, about 650g/1¼ lb each
60–90 g/2–3 oz/¼–⅓ cup butter
3 tbsp drained capers
2 tbsp wine vinegar
1 tbsp chopped fresh parsley
salt and pepper

TO GARNISH:
lime or lemon slices or wedges
sprigs of fresh parsley

1 Wash the skate wings, dry and then cut each in half. Place in a roasting tin (pan) in a single layer and cover with salted water.

2 Bring to the boil, cover with foil or a baking sheet (cookie sheet) and simmer gently for 10–15 minutes until tender.

3 Drain the fish thoroughly and place on a warm dish; keep warm.

4 Melt the butter in a small saucepan then continue to cook until it turns golden brown (taking care it does not burn and turn black).

5 Quickly add the capers and vinegar and cook until bubbling. Season lightly and stir in the chopped parsley.

6 Spoon the sauce over the skate and serve garnished with lime or lemon and parsley sprigs.

ACCOMPANIMENTS

Boiled new or mashed potatoes make a good accompaniment, together with a green vegetable such as peas, mangetout (snow peas) or French (green) beans.

VARIATIONS

For a creamier sauce, stir in 4 tablespoons of single (light) cream or fromage frais with the parsley.

The sauce is excellent served with other white fish, such as cod, haddock, sole, halibut, turbot or plaice; they can be poached, grilled (broiled) or baked.

STEP 2

STEP 4

STEP 5

STEP 5

KEDGEREE

This old favourite is traditionally made with smoked haddock and flavoured with parsley, but tarragon makes an interesting variation. Other fish, such as fresh or smoked salmon, kippers or tuna, make excellent alternatives.

SERVES 4

300 g/10 oz/scant 1½ cups long-grain rice
375 g/12 oz smoked haddock fillet
1 bay leaf
2–3 lemon slices
60 g/2 oz/¼ cup butter or margarine
1 large onion, chopped finely
125 g/4 oz/2 cups button mushrooms, sliced (optional)
good pinch of ground coriander
3 tbsp chopped fresh parsley or 2 tbsp chopped fresh tarragon
2–4 hard-boiled (hard-cooked) eggs, chopped
6–8 tbsp single (light) cream
salt and pepper

TO GARNISH:
sprigs of fresh parsley or tarragon
chopped fresh parsley

1 Cook the rice in boiling salted water until just tender. Drain, rinse under hot water and drain well.

2 Put the fish in a saucepan and barely cover with water. Add the bay leaf and lemon slices and poach gently for about 15 minutes until tender. Drain thoroughly, remove the skin and any bones from the fish and flake the fish.

3 Melt the butter or margarine in a saucepan and fry the onion gently until soft and just barely coloured. Add the mushrooms, if using, and cook for 2–3 minutes.

4 Add the flaked haddock, the coriander and plenty of seasoning and heat through, stirring frequently.

5 Add the cooked rice, parsley or tarragon and eggs and heat through, stirring from time to time. Pour the cream over, mix lightly and serve, garnished with sprigs of parsley or tarragon and chopped parsley.

FREEZING

Kedgeree can be frozen for up to 2 months, but do not add the hard-boiled (hard-cooked) eggs and cream until just before serving.

VARIATIONS

Tarragon blends well with flaked fresh or smoked salmon; parsley or thyme go well with kippers (use boned fillets); and most herbs complement canned tuna.

STEP 1

STEP 3

STEP 4

STEP 6

OCEAN PIE

A tasty fish pie combining a mixture of fish and shellfish. You can use a wide variety of fish – whatever is available.

SERVES 4

500 g / 1 lb cod or haddock fillet, skinned
250 g / 8 oz salmon steak
450 ml / ³/₄ pint / scant 2 cups milk
1 bay leaf
1 kg / 2 lb potatoes
60 g / 2 oz / ¹/₃ cup peeled prawns (shrimp),
*   thawed if frozen*
60 g / 2 oz / ¹/₄ cup butter or margarine
30 g / 1 oz / 4 tbsp plain (all-purpose) flour
2–4 tbsp white wine
1 tsp chopped fresh dill or ¹/₂ tsp dried dill
2 tbsp drained capers
salt and pepper
few whole prawns (shrimp) in their shells,
*   to garnish*

1 Put the cod or haddock and salmon into a saucepan with 300 ml/ ¹/₂ pint/1 ¹/₄ cups of the milk, the bay leaf and seasoning. Bring to the boil, cover and simmer gently for 10–15 minutes until tender.

2 Meanwhile, coarsely chop the potatoes and cook in boiling salted water until tender.

3 Drain the fish, reserving 300 ml/ ¹/₂ pint/1 ¹/₄ cups of the cooking liquid (make up with more milk if

necessary). Flake the fish, discarding any bones and place in a shallow ovenproof dish. Add the prawns (shrimp).

4 Melt half the butter or margarine in a saucepan, add the flour and cook, stirring, for a minute or so. Gradually stir in the reserved stock and the wine and bring to the boil. Add the herbs, capers and seasoning to taste and simmer until thickened. Pour over the fish and mix well.

5 Drain the potatoes and mash, adding the remaining butter or margarine, seasoning and sufficient milk to give a piping consistency.

6 Put the mashed potato into a piping bag fitted with a large star nozzle (tip) and pipe whirls over the fish to cover completely. Cook in a preheated oven at 200°C/400°F/Gas Mark 6 for about 25 minutes until piping hot and browned. Serve garnished with whole prawns (shrimp).

CHAPTER THREE

Meat & Game

In this chapter I have included favourite recipes that are suitable for both everyday meals and entertaining.

Boiled Beef, or salt beef as it is sometimes known, is a joint of topside or silverside which has been soaked in a brine solution for about a week, then gently simmered (not boiled, which toughens the meat) with root vegetables and dumplings. Beef features again in Steak and Kidney Pudding, where it is cut into small pieces to ensure that it is completely tender. Extra flavourings such as oysters (the traditional ingredient), mushrooms or fresh herbs can be added to vary the basic recipe.

Cooking vegetables with meat adds flavour and often makes the dish a complete meal. Creamed potato is used to top Shepherd's Pie, while slices of potato are baked on top of a Savoury Hotpot. Both recipes also combine a mixture of onions, carrots and other vegetables.

A good sauce can transform a simple meal: Cumberland Sauce is the perfect tangy partner for Baked Ham and can also be served as an alternative accompaniment for Roast Pheasant.

Opposite: *Different cuts of lamb feature in a number of classic recipes – from cutlets or chops in Savoury Hotpot to minced (ground) lamb in Shepherd's Pie.*

BOILED BEEF & CARROTS
WITH DUMPLINGS

*A real old favourite using a salted joint of silverside or topside. Serve
with vegetables and herby dumplings for a substantial one-pot meal.*

STEP 1

STEP 3

STEP 4

STEP 5

SERVES 6

about 1.75 kg/3½ lb joint of salted
   silverside or topside
2 onions, quartered, or 5–8 small onions
8–10 cloves
2 bay leaves
1 cinnamon stick
2 tbsp brown sugar
4 large carrots, sliced thickly
1 turnip, quartered
½ swede, sliced thickly
1 large leek, sliced thickly
30 g/1 oz/2 tbsp butter or margarine
30 g/1 oz/4 tbsp plain (all-purpose) flour
½ tsp dried mustard powder
salt and pepper

DUMPLINGS:
250 g/8 oz/2 cups self-raising flour
½ tsp dried sage
90 g/3 oz/generous ½ cup shredded suet
about 150 ml/¼ pint/⅔ cup water

1 Put the beef in a large saucepan,
add the onions, cloves, bay leaves,
cinnamon and sugar and sufficient water
to cover the meat.

2 Bring slowly to the boil, remove
any scum from the surface, cover
and simmer gently for 1 hour.

3 Add the carrots, turnip, swede and
leeks, cover and simmer for a
further 1¼ hours until the beef is tender.

4 Meanwhile, make the dumplings.
Sift the flour into a bowl, season
well and mix in the herbs and suet. Add
sufficient water to mix to a softish dough.

5 Divide the dough into 8 pieces,
roughly shape into balls and place
on top of the beef and vegetables. Replace
the lid and simmer for 15–20 minutes
until the dumplings are well puffed up
and cooked.

6 Remove the dumplings, then place
the beef and vegetables in a serving
dish. Measure 300 ml/½ pint/1¼ cups of
the cooking liquid into a saucepan. Blend
the butter or margarine with the flour
then gradually whisk into the pan. Bring
to the boil and simmer until thickened.
Stir in the mustard, adjust the seasoning
and serve with the beef.

STEP 1

STEP 2

STEP 3

STEP 4

SAVOURY HOTPOT

A hearty lamb stew full of vegetables and herbs and topped with a layer of crisp, golden potato slices.

SERVES 4

8 middle neck lamb chops, neck of lamb or
*   any stewing lamb on the bone*
1–2 garlic cloves, crushed
2 lamb's kidneys (optional)
1 large onion, sliced thinly
1 leek, sliced
2–3 carrots, sliced
1 tsp chopped fresh tarragon or sage or
*   ½ tsp dried tarragon or sage*
1 kg/2 lb potatoes, sliced thinly
300 ml/½ pint/1¼ cups stock
30 g/1 oz/2 tbsp butter or margarine,
*   melted, or 1 tbsp vegetable oil*
salt and pepper
chopped fresh parsley to garnish

1 Trim the lamb of any excess fat, season well with salt and pepper and arrange in a large ovenproof casserole. Sprinkle with the garlic.

2 If using kidneys, remove the skin, halve the kidneys and cut out the cores. Chop into small pieces and sprinkle over the lamb.

3 Place the onion, leek and carrots over the lamb, allowing the pieces to slip in between the meat, then sprinkle with the herbs.

4 Arrange the potatoes evenly over the contents of the casserole. Bring the stock to the boil, season and pour into the casserole.

5 Brush the potatoes with melted butter or margarine, or oil, cover with greased foil or a lid and cook in a preheated oven at 180°C/350°F/Gas Mark 4 for 1½ hours.

6 Remove the foil or lid from the potatoes, increase the oven temperature to 220°C/425°F/Gas Mark 7 and return the casserole to the oven for about 30 minutes until the potatoes are browned. Garnish with chopped parsley.

VARIATION

Small pieces of chicken, such as thighs or drumsticks, may also be cooked this way.

STEP 2

STEP 3

STEP 5

STEP 6

SHEPHERD'S PIE

Minced (ground) lamb or beef cooked with onions, carrots, herbs and tomatoes and with a topping of piped creamed potatoes.

SERVES 4–5

*750 g/1½ lb lean minced (ground) or lamb
  or beef
2 onions, chopped
250 g/8 oz carrots, diced
1–2 garlic cloves, crushed
1 tbsp plain (all-purpose) flour
200 ml/7 fl oz/scant 1 cup beef stock
200 g/7 oz can chopped tomatoes
1 tsp Worcestershire sauce
1 tsp chopped fresh sage or oregano or ½ tsp
  dried sage or oregano
750 g–1 kg/1½–2 lb potatoes
30 g/1 oz/2 tbsp butter or margarine
3–4 tbsp milk
125 g/4 oz button mushrooms, sliced
  (optional)
salt and pepper*

1 Place the meat in a heavy-based saucepan with no extra fat and cook gently, stirring frequently, until the meat begins to brown.

2 Add the onions, carrots and garlic and continue to cook gently for about 10 minutes. Stir in the flour and cook for a minute or so, then gradually stir in the stock and tomatoes and bring to the boil.

3 Add the Worcestershire sauce, seasoning and herbs, cover the pan and simmer gently for about 25 minutes, giving an occasional stir.

4 Cook the potatoes in boiling salted water until tender, then drain thoroughly and mash, beating in the butter or margarine, seasoning and sufficient milk to give a piping consistency. Place in a piping bag fitted with a large star nozzle (tip).

5 Stir the mushrooms, if using, into the meat and adjust the seasoning. Turn into a shallow ovenproof dish.

6 Pipe the potatoes evenly over the meat. Cook in a preheated oven at 200°C/400°F/Gas Mark 6 for about 30 minutes until piping hot and the potatoes are golden brown.

VARIATIONS

If liked, a mixture of boiled potatoes and parsnips or swede may be used for the topping.
Sprinkle the top with 2 tbsp grated Cheddar cheese before baking, if liked.

STEAK & KIDNEY PUDDING

This well-loved savoury suet pudding is packed full of steak and kidney with either oysters or mushrooms for extra flavour. Use best quality beef and chop it finely so it becomes really tender when steamed.

STEP 2

STEP 3

STEP 4

SERVES 4

500 g/1 lb best braising steak, trimmed
175 g/6 oz ox or lamb's kidneys
2 tbsp seasoned plain (all-purpose) flour
125 g/4 oz/2 cups button mushrooms,
   sliced or quartered or a small can oysters
   or smoked oysters, drained
about 4 tbsp red wine, beef stock or water
$^1/_2$ tsp Worcestershire sauce
$^1/_2$ tsp dried mixed herbs
salt and pepper
sprigs of fresh parsley to garnish

SUET CRUST PASTRY (PIE DOUGH):
250 g/8 oz/2 cups self-raising flour
$^1/_2$ tsp salt
125 g/4 oz/$^2/_3$ cup shredded suet
about 150 ml/$^1/_4$ pint/$^2/_3$ cup cold water

1 Grease a 1 litre/2 pint/5 cup pudding basin (mold). To make the pastry (pie dough), sift the flour and salt into a bowl and stir in the suet. Add sufficient water to mix to a soft dough and knead lightly. Roll out three-quarters of the pastry (pie dough) to about 5 mm/$^1/_4$ inch thick and use to line the basin (mold).

2 Cut the steak into 2 cm/$^3/_4$ inch cubes. Skin the kidneys, remove

the cores and cut into small cubes. Toss the meats in the seasoned flour.

3 Put the meat in the basin (mold), layering it with the mushrooms or oysters and seasoning, if required. Combine the wine, stock or water, Worcestershire sauce and herbs and add to the basin (mold).

4 Roll out the remaining pastry (pie dough) to form a lid, dampen the edges and position, pressing the edges firmly together. Trim.

5 Cover with a piece of pleated greased baking parchment and then with pleated foil, and tie very securely under the rim of the basin.

6 Put in a saucepan with enough boiling water to reach halfway up the basin (mold), or in the top of a steamer. Cover and steam for about 4 hours, adding more boiling water to the saucepan as necessary.

7 To serve the pudding, remove the cloth or foil and paper, tie a napkin around the bowl and serve from the basin (mold) – it may split open if you turn it out first.

STEP 5

STEP 1

STEP 2

STEP 3

STEP 5

BAKED HAM WITH CUMBERLAND SAUCE

A joint of gammon or collar bacon is first par-boiled then baked with a mustard topping. Serve hot or cold with this tangy Cumberland sauce.

SERVES 4–6

2–3 kg/4–6 lb gammon or prime collar joint
  of bacon
2 bay leaves
1–2 onions, quartered
2 carrots, sliced thickly
6 cloves

GLAZE:
1 tbsp redcurrant jelly
1 tbsp wholegrain mustard

CUMBERLAND SAUCE:
1 orange
3 tbsp redcurrant jelly
2 tbsp lemon or lime juice
2 tbsp orange juice
2–4 tbsp port
1 tbsp wholegrain mustard

TO GARNISH:
salad leaves
orange slices

1 Put the meat in a large saucepan. Add the bay leaves, onion, carrots and cloves and cover with cold water. Bring slowly to the boil, cover and simmer for half the cooking time, allowing 30 minutes per 500 g/1 lb plus 30 minutes.

2 Drain the meat and remove the skin. Put the meat in a roasting tin (pan) or dish and score the fat.

3 To make the glaze, combine the ingredients and spread over the fat. Cook in a preheated oven at 180°C/ 350°F/Gas Mark 4 for the remainder of the cooking time. Baste at least once.

4 To make the sauce, thinly pare the rind from half the orange and cut into narrow strips. Cook in boiling water for 3 minutes then drain.

5 Place all the remaining sauce ingredients in a small saucepan and heat gently until the redcurrant jelly dissolves. Add the orange rind and simmer gently for 3–4 minutes. Slice the gammon or bacon and serve with the Cumberland sauce, garnished with salad leaves and orange slices

SOAKING

It is a good idea to soak the joint in cold water for at least 2 or 3 hours, preferably overnight, especially if it is smoked. This removes excess salt.

STEP 1

STEP 2

STEP 3

STEP 5

ROAST PHEASANT WITH TANGY CRANBERRY SAUCE

Small, young pheasants are far more tender than larger ones, so for a family meal, roast a brace (two). Serve with this cranberry sauce, and the traditional accompaniments of Fried Breadcrumbs and Bread Sauce.

SERVES 4–6

1 brace oven-ready pheasants
1 lemon, quartered
4 tbsp melted dripping or butter, or vegetable oil
8 slices streaky bacon, derinded
salt and pepper
watercress to garnish

TANGY CRANBERRY SAUCE:
1 tbsp plain (all-purpose) flour
150 ml/¼ pint/²/₃ cup stock
150 ml/¼ pint/²/₃ cup red wine
finely pared rind and juice of 1 orange
4 tbsp cranberry sauce
125 g/4 oz shelled chestnuts, roasted and boiled, or canned chestnuts (optional)

TO SERVE:
Fried Breadcrumbs (see page 79)
Bread Sauce (see page 79)

1 Wipe the pheasants inside and out and place in a roasting tin (pan). Put half the butter and 2 slices of lemon in each cavity. Tie the legs together.

2 Brush 2 tablespoons of melted dripping or butter, or oil over each bird and season lightly. Lay the bacon slices over the breasts.

3 Roast in a preheated oven at 220°C/425°F/Gas Mark 7 for ¾–1¼ hours depending on the size of the birds, basting regularly until just cooked through and tender. Do not overcook or the flesh will become tough. Transfer the pheasants to a serving dish and keep warm.

4 To make the tangy cranberry sauce, discard all but 2 tablespoons of the juices from the roasting tin (pan). Add the flour to the tin (pan) and cook, stirring, for a minute or so. Gradually stir in the stock and wine and bring to the boil, stirring until thickened.

5 Strain into a saucepan and add the orange rind and juice, the cranberry sauce and chestnuts, if using. Simmer for 3–4 minutes and adjust the seasoning. Garnish the pheasants with watercress and serve with the sauce, accompanied by fried breadcrumbs and bread sauce.

CHAPTER FOUR

Snacks & Light Meals

In the busy lives we lead today, quick meals are becoming great favourites. But if we eat snacks, or 'food on the move', great care must be taken to ensure it is properly prepared and cooked, well-balanced and not just 'junk' food so that the diet is not harmed nor do we lose the tradition of the family meal.

Snacks and easy meals can be quickly prepared using a variety of foods to suit all tastes, including meat-eaters, vegetarians, children and teenagers. Toad in the Hole, for instance, which can be made in individual dishes or one large dish, makes an excellent snack, as do Buck Rarebit and Fish Cakes. Scalloped Potatoes makes a very good vegetable accompaniment as well as a snack meal.

Pasties and pies are well known as snack foods and are also useful for taking on picnics or including in packed lunches. Fillings for pies and pasties can vary enormously, ranging from the minced (ground) meat and vegetables in Cornish Pasties to the unusual blend of artichokes, grapes, onions, hard-boiled (hard-cooked) eggs and dates in Elizabethan Artichoke Pie.

Opposite: Eggs are a natural and nutritious 'fast food' and feature in many snacks and light meals.

STEP 1

STEP 4

STEP 5

STEP 6

TOAD IN THE HOLE

A real old family favourite combining sausages and batter. It is traditionally baked in one large dish but in this recipe small Yorkshire pudding tins (muffin pans) are used to make individual servings.

SERVES 4

125 g/4 oz/1 cup plain (all-purpose) flour
¹/₂ tsp salt
2 eggs
275 ml/9 fl oz/scant 1¹/₄ cups milk
³/₄ tsp dried mixed herbs or an individual
*   herb (optional)*
2 tbsp vegetable oil or dripping
1 onion, chopped finely
8 sausages, about 500 g/1 lb

1 Sift the flour and salt into a bowl and make a well in the centre. Add the eggs and about one-third of the milk and gradually work in the flour, beating until smooth.

2 Gradually beat in the rest of the milk. Add the herbs, if using.

3 Use the oil or dripping to thoroughly grease 8 x 10–12 cm/4–4¹/₂ inch individual Yorkshire pudding tins (muffin pans) or a shallow ovenproof dish or roasting tin (pan).

4 Divide the onion between the tins (pans) then put a sausage in each tin (pan) and prick well. If using a large dish or tin (pan), add the onion and arrange the sausages in it.

5 Cook in a preheated oven at 220°C/425°F/Gas Mark 7 for 8–10 minutes until the sausages are beginning to colour a little, then stir the batter well and divide between the tins (pans) or pour evenly into the dish or tin (pan).

6 Return to the oven for 20–25 minutes until the batter is well risen and golden brown. The larger dish or tin (pan) will take 40–45 minutes.

ACCOMPANIMENTS

Gravy or a white or parsley sauce, creamed potatoes and a green vegetable are good accompaniments.

SAUSAGES

Any type of sausages can be used: plain pork, pork with herbs, beef, pork and beef, turkey or vegetarian, but large sausages are better than chipolatas.

SCALLOPED POTATOES

*Layers of sliced potatoes with onions and diced bacon and a crispy
browned cheese topping. This dish can be cooked with stock for
everyday meals or with cream if you want to make it more special.*

STEP 2

SERVES 4

1.25 kg/2¹/₂ lb potatoes
2 large onions, chopped finely
2 garlic cloves, crushed (optional)
175–250 g/6–8 oz lean bacon, derinded
*   and diced*
2 tbsp chopped fresh dill or ³/₄ tsp dried dill
450 ml/³/₄ pint/scant 2 cups stock, milk or
*   single (light) cream*
15 g/¹/₂ oz/1 tbsp butter or margarine,
*   melted*
60 g/2 oz/¹/₂ cup mature (sharp) Cheddar,
*   Gouda (Dutch) or Emmenthal (Swiss)*
*   cheese, grated*
salt and pepper

1 Slice the potatoes, either by hand
or using a food processor.

2 Thoroughly grease a large
ovenproof dish or roasting tin
(pan). Arrange a layer of sliced potatoes
in the dish or tin (pan) and sprinkle with
half the onions. Season lightly.

3 Add a second layer of potatoes,
then the rest of the onions, the
garlic, if using, the bacon, dill and
seasoning, sprinkling evenly. Add a final
layer of potatoes, arranging them in an
attractive pattern.

4 Gently heat the stock, milk or
cream and pour over the potatoes.
Brush the top layer of potatoes with the
melted butter or margarine and cover
with greased foil or a lid.

5 Cook in a preheated oven at
200°C/400°F/Gas Mark 6 for
1 hour.

6 Remove the foil or lid and sprinkle
the cheese over the potatoes.
Return, uncovered, to the oven for a
further 30–45 minutes until well
browned on top and the potatoes are
tender.

STEP 3

STEP 4

VARIATIONS

Chopped salami, garlic sausage, diced
smoked salmon or sliced button
mushrooms may be used in place of the
bacon in this dish.

STEP 6

STEP 2

STEP 3

STEP 4

STEP 5

CORNISH PASTIES

Although Cornish pasties usually have a meaty filling, they originally contained a savoury filling at one end and a sweet one at the other – providing a complete meal in a convenient package.

SERVES 4

175 g/6 oz/³/₄ cup extra lean minced
 (ground) beef or lamb
1 onion, chopped finely
1 garlic clove, crushed
1 small carrot, chopped very finely
125 g/4 oz potato, chopped very finely or
 grated coarsely
¹/₂ tsp dried mixed herbs or thyme, tarragon,
 sage or oregano
salt and pepper

SHORTCRUST PASTRY (PIE DOUGH):
250 g/8 oz/2 cups plain (all-purpose) flour
good pinch of salt
60 g/2 oz/¹/₄ cup butter or margarine
60 g/2 oz/¹/₄ cup lard or white vegetable fat
 (shortening)
about 4 tbsp cold water
beaten egg or milk to glaze

TO SERVE:
salad leaves
cherry tomatoes

1 To make the pastry (pie dough), sift the flour and salt into a bowl, rub in the butter or margarine and lard or white fat (shortening) until the mixture resembles fine breadcrumbs, then add sufficient water to mix to a pliable dough.

Knead lightly. Wrap in foil or clingfilm (plastic wrap) and chill for 30 minutes.

2 Combine the meat, onion, garlic, carrot, potato, herbs and seasoning. Divide into 4 portions.

3 Roll out the pastry (pie dough) and, using a saucer or plate, cut into 4 × 18–20 cm/7–8 inch rounds.

4 Place a portion of the meat mixture in the centre of each round.

5 Dampen the edges of the pastry (pie dough) and bring together at the top. Press the edges together and crimp.

6 Put the pasties on a greased baking sheet (cookie sheet) and glaze with beaten egg or milk. Bake in a preheated oven at 220°C/425°F/Gas Mark 7 for about 30 minutes until golden. Serve hot or cold, with salad leaves and tomatoes.

VARIATIONS

All kinds of ingredients make good fillings for pasties. Add finely chopped leeks, mushrooms or tomatoes, or replace the beef or lamb with chopped chicken or fish.

FISH CAKES WITH SPICY SAUCE

A smoky flavour gives these fish cakes a special tang, making them very popular with children and adults alike. The spicy sauce is a good way to liven up bottled ketchup.

STEP 3

STEP 4

STEP 5

STEP 6

SERVES 4

1 kg/2 lb potatoes, cut into chunks
350–500 g/³/₄–1 lb smoked haddock or cod fillet, skinned
1 bay leaf
2 hard-boiled (hard-cooked) eggs, chopped finely
2–3 tbsp chopped fresh parsley
1 tbsp chopped fresh tarragon or 1 tsp dried tarragon
2–3 spring onions (scallions), chopped (optional)
30 g/1 oz/2 tbsp butter or margarine
1 egg, beaten
dried white or golden breadcrumbs
salt and pepper
vegetable oil for brushing or frying

SPICY SAUCE:
150 ml/¹/₄ pint/²/₃ cup dry white wine
150 ml/¹/₄ pint/²/₃ cup tomato ketchup
1–2 garlic cloves, crushed
good dash of Worcestershire sauce

TO GARNISH:
sprigs of fresh parsley
lemon slices

1 Cook the potatoes in boiling salted water until tender.

2 Meanwhile, put the fish and bay leaf in a saucepan and barely cover with water. Bring to the boil, cover and simmer for 15 minutes until tender.

3 Drain the fish, remove the skin and any bones and flake. Put in a bowl with the eggs, herbs, spring onions (scallions), if using, and seasoning and mix well.

4 Drain the potatoes and mash with the butter and seasoning. Add to the fish and mix thoroughly.

5 Divide the mixture into 8 and shape into cakes. Brush with beaten egg then coat in breadcrumbs. Put on a greased baking sheet (cookie sheet), brush with oil and cook in a preheated oven at 200°C/400°F/Gas Mark 6 for about 30 minutes until golden. Alternatively, fry for about 5 minutes on each side.

6 To make the spicy sauce, put all the ingredients in a saucepan, bring to the boil and simmer, uncovered, for about 15 minutes until thickened and smooth. Adjust the seasoning. Serve with the fish cakes, garnished with parsley and lemon.

STEP 2

STEP 3

STEP 4

STEP 6

BUCK RAREBIT

*This substantial version of cheese on toast – a creamy cheese sauce
topped with a poached egg – makes a tasty, filling snack.*

SERVES 4

350 g/12 oz mature (sharp) Cheddar cheese
125 g/4 oz Gouda (Dutch), Gruyère or
*   Emmenthal (Swiss) cheese*
1 tsp mustard powder
1 tsp wholegrain mustard
2–4 tbsp brown ale, cider or milk
1/2 tsp Worcestershire sauce
4 thick slices white or brown bread
4 eggs
salt and pepper

TO GARNISH:
tomato wedges
watercress sprigs

1 Grate the cheeses and place in a saucepan, preferably non-stick.

2 Add the mustards, seasoning, brown ale, cider or milk and Worcestershire sauce and mix well.

3 Heat the cheese mixture gently, stirring, until it has melted and is completely creamy and thick. Remove from the heat and leave to cool a little.

4 Toast the slices of bread on each side under a preheated grill (broiler) then spread the rarebit mixture evenly over each piece. Put under a moderate grill (broiler) until golden brown and bubbling.

5 Meanwhile, poach the eggs. If using a poacher, grease the cups, heat the water in the pan and, when just boiling, break the eggs into the cups. Cover and simmer for 4–5 minutes until just set. Alternatively, bring about 4 cm/1½ inches of water to the boil in a frying pan (skillet) or large saucepan and for each egg quickly swirl the water with a knife and drop the egg into the 'hole' created. Cook for about 4 minutes until just set.

6 Top the rarebits with a poached egg and serve garnished with tomato and sprigs of watercress.

VARIATION

For a change, you can use part or all Stilton or other blue cheese; the appearance is not so attractive but the flavour is very good.

ELIZABETHAN ARTICHOKE PIE

A traditional double-crust vegetable pie. The filling of Jerusalem artichokes, grapes, onion, dates and hard-boiled (hard-cooked) eggs is an unusual but delicious blend of flavours.

STEP 2

STEP 3

STEP 4

STEP 5

SERVES 4–6

350 g/12 oz Jerusalem artichokes
30 g/1 oz/2 tbsp butter or margarine
1 onion, chopped
1–2 garlic cloves, crushed
125 g/4 oz white (green) seedless grapes,
    halved
60 g/2 oz/¹/₃ cup dates, chopped coarsely
2 hard-boiled (hard-cooked) eggs, sliced
1 tbsp chopped fresh mixed herbs or 1 tsp
    dried herbs
4–6 tbsp single (light) cream or natural
    yogurt

SHORTCRUST PASTRY (PIE DOUGH):
350 g/12 oz/3 cups plain (all-purpose)
    flour
good pinch of salt
90 g/3 oz/¹/₃ cup butter or margarine
90 g/3 oz/¹/₃ cup lard or white vegetable fat
    (shortening)
4–6 tbsp cold water
beaten egg or milk to glaze

1 To make the pastry (pie dough), see Cornish Pasties (page 54).

2 Peel the artichokes, plunging them immediately into salted water to prevent discolouration. Drain, cover with fresh water, bring to the boil and simmer for 10–12 minutes until just tender. Drain well.

3 Heat the butter or margarine in a saucepan and fry the onion and garlic until soft but not coloured. Remove the pan from the heat and stir in the grapes and dates.

4 Roll out almost two-thirds of the pastry (pie dough) and use to line a 20 cm/8 inch pie dish. Slice the artichokes and arrange in the pie dish, cover with slices of egg and then with the onion mixture, seasoning and herbs.

5 Roll out the remaining pastry (pie dough), dampen the edges and use to cover the pie; press the edges firmly together, then trim and crimp. Roll out the trimmings and cut into narrow strips. Arrange a lattice over the top of the pie, dampening the strips to attach them.

6 Glaze with beaten egg or milk and make 2–3 slits in the lid. Bake in a preheated oven at 200°C/400°F/Gas Mark 6 for 40–50 minutes until golden. Gently heat the cream or yogurt and pour into the pie through the holes in the lid. Serve hot or cold.

CHAPTER FIVE

Desserts

Not everyone has a sweet tooth or is a great pudding fanatic, but most people will have a longing for some type of sweet from time to time, and a dessert is always a good way to round off a special meal.

Here is a selection of all-time classics. A Traditional Apple Pie with its spicy filling will simply melt in the mouth whether served hot or cold, and you can serve it with cream, yogurt, custard, ice cream or just on its own. Bread and Butter Pudding has been a favourite through the years and there are many different recipes – for simple and for rich versions. My pudding is enhanced with grated citrus rinds, dried fruits and chunky marmalade for an extra special taste. Bread is also used to make Summer Pudding – summer fruits are encased in slices of bread which soak up the wonderful red juices. Syllabub is a real old-fashioned dessert that dates back to the Middle Ages. A steamed pudding has to feature in this book, and the one I have chosen contains dried fruits, ginger, orange rind, grated apple and a layer of golden (light corn) syrup – delicious, but not for serious weight-watchers.

Opposite: *Apples are always a favourite dessert, whether cooked in crisp, shortcrust pastry (pie dough) or topped with a crunchy layer of crumble.*

STEP 1

STEP 3

STEP 4

STEP 6

SPICED STEAMED PUDDING

Steamed puddings are irresistible on a winter's day but the texture of this pudding is so light it can be served throughout the year.

SERVES 4–6

2 tbsp golden (light corn) syrup
125 g/4 oz/½ cup butter or margarine
125 g/4 oz/generous ½ cup caster
   (superfine) or light soft brown sugar
2 eggs
175 g/6 oz/1½ cups self-raising flour
¾ tsp ground cinnamon or mixed spice
grated rind of 1 orange
1 tbsp orange juice
90 g/3 oz/½ cup sultanas (golden raisins)
   or raisins
45 g/1½ oz/5 tbsp stem (candied) ginger,
   chopped finely
1 dessert (eating) apple, peeled, cored and
   grated coarsely
extra golden (light corn) syrup, warmed, to
   serve

1 Thoroughly grease a 900 ml/1½ pint/3¾ cup pudding basin (mold). Put the golden (light corn) syrup into the basin (mold).

2 Cream the butter or margarine and sugar together until very light and fluffy and pale in colour. Beat in the eggs, one at a time, following each with a spoonful of the flour.

3 Sift the remaining flour with the cinnamon or spice and fold into the mixture, followed by the orange rind and juice. Fold in the sultanas (golden raisins) or raisins then the ginger and apple.

4 Turn the mixture into the basin (mold) and level the top. Cover with a piece of pleated greased baking parchment, tucking the edges under the rim of the basin (mold).

5 Cover with a sheet of pleated foil. Tie in place with string, with a piece of string tied over the top of the basin (mold) for a handle.

6 Put the basin (mold) into a saucepan half filled with boiling water, cover and steam for 1½ hours, adding more boiling water to the pan as necessary during cooking.

7 To serve, remove the foil and baking parchment, turn the pudding on to a warmed serving plate and serve with warmed golden (light corn) syrup.

STEP 2

STEP 3

STEP 4

STEP 5

RHUBARB & ORANGE CRUMBLE

*A mixture of rhubarb and apples flavoured with orange rind, brown
sugar and spices and topped with a crunchy crumble topping
containing chopped hazelnuts.*

SERVES 4–6

500 g/1 lb rhubarb
500 g/1 lb cooking apples
grated rind and juice of 1 orange
1/2–1 tsp ground cinnamon
about 90 g/3 oz/scant 1/2 cup light soft
  brown sugar

CRUMBLE:
250 g/8 oz/2 cups plain (all-purpose) flour
125 g/4 oz/1/2 cup butter or margarine
125 g/4 oz/generous 1/2 cup light soft brown
  or demerara (brown crystal) sugar
45–60 g/11/2–2 oz/1/3–1/2 cup toasted
  chopped hazelnuts
2 tbsp demerara sugar (optional)

1 Cut the rhubarb into 2.5 cm/
1 inch lengths and place in a large
saucepan.

2 Peel, core and slice the apples and
add to the rhubarb with the grated
orange rind and juice. Bring to the boil
and simmer for 2–3 minutes until the
fruit begins to soften.

3 Add the cinnamon and sugar to
taste and turn the mixture into an
ovenproof dish, so it is not more than
two-thirds full.

4 Sift the flour into a bowl and rub in
the butter or margarine until the
mixture resembles fine breadcrumbs (this
can be done by hand or in a food
processor). Stir in the sugar followed by
the nuts.

5 Spoon the crumble mixture evenly
over the fruit in the dish and level
the top. Sprinkle with demerara (brown
crystal) sugar, if liked.

6 Cook in a preheated oven at 200°C/
400°F/Gas Mark 6 for 30–40
minutes until the topping is browned.
Serve hot or cold.

VARIATIONS

Other flavourings such as 60 g/2 oz/
generous 1/4 cup chopped stem (candied)
ginger can be added either to the fruit or
the crumb mixture.
  Any fruit, or mixtures of fruit, such as
apple, blackberry, apricot, cherry
blackcurrant, raspberry or gooseberry can
be topped with crumble.

STEP 2

STEP 3

STEP 5

STEP 6

BREAD & BUTTER PUDDING

Everyone has their own favourite recipe for this dish. Mine has added marmalade and grated apples for a really rich and unique taste. Serve with cream, natural yogurt or custard, if liked.

SERVES 4–6

about 60 g/2 oz/¼ cup butter, softened
4–5 slices white or brown bread
4 tbsp chunky orange marmalade
grated rind of 1 lemon
90–125 g/3–4 oz/½–¾ cup raisins or
    sultanas (golden raisins)
45 g/1½ oz/¼ cup chopped mixed (candied)
    peel
1 tsp ground cinnamon or mixed spice
1 cooking apple, peeled, cored and grated
    coarsely
90 g/3 oz/scant ½ cup demerara (golden
    crystal) or light soft brown sugar
3 eggs
500 ml/16 fl oz/2 cups milk
2 tbsp demerara (brown crystal) sugar

1 Use the butter to grease an ovenproof dish and to spread on the slices of bread, then spread the bread with the marmalade.

2 Place a layer of bread in the base of the dish and sprinkle with the lemon rind, half the raisins or sultanas (golden raisins), half the peel, half the spice, all of the apple and half the sugar.

3 Add another layer of bread, cutting so it fits the dish.

4 Sprinkle over most of the remaining raisins or sultanas (golden raisins) and the remaining peel, spice and sugar, sprinkling it evenly over the bread. Top with a final layer of bread, again cutting to fit the dish.

5 Beat together the eggs and milk and then strain over the bread in the dish. If time allows, leave to stand for 20–30 minutes.

6 Sprinkle with the demerara (brown crystal) sugar and the remaining raisins or sultanas (golden raisins) and cook in a preheated oven at 200°C/400°F/Gas Mark 6 for 50–60 minutes until risen and golden brown. Serve hot or cold.

VARIATIONS

You can replace the slices of bread with thinly sliced French bread or brioche, if you prefer.

For a quicker version of this pudding, omit the raisins and mixed (candied) peel, and replace the white or brown bread with slices of tea bread.

STEP 2

STEP 3

STEP 4

STEP 5

TRADITIONAL APPLE PIE

This apple pie recipe has a double crust and can be served either hot or cold. The apples can be flavoured with other spices or the grated rind of an orange or lemon, if liked.

SERVES 4–6

750 g–1 kg/1¹/₂–2 lb cooking apples, peeled, cored and sliced
about 125 g/4 oz/generous ¹/₂ cup brown or white sugar, plus extra for sprinkling
¹/₂–1 tsp ground cinnamon, mixed spice or ginger
1–2 tbsp water

SHORTCRUST PASTRY (PIE DOUGH):
350 g/12 oz/3 cups plain (all-purpose) flour
good pinch of salt
90 g/3 oz/¹/₃ cup butter or margarine
90 g/3 oz/¹/₃ cup lard or white vegetable fat (shortening)
about 6 tbsp cold water
beaten egg or top of the milk for glazing

1 To make the pastry (pie dough), see Cornish Pasties (page 54). If time allows, wrap in foil or clingfilm (plastic wrap) and chill for 30 minutes.

2 Roll out almost two-thirds of the pastry (pie dough) thinly and use to line a 20–23 cm/8–9 inch deep pie plate or shallow pie tin (pan).

3 Mix the apples with the sugar and spice and pack into the pastry case

(pie shell); the filling can come up above the rim. Add the water if liked, particularly if the apples are a dry variety.

4 Roll out the remaining pastry (pie dough) to form a lid (top). Dampen the edges of the pie rim with water and position the lid (top), pressing the edges firmly together. Trim and crimp the edges.

5 Use the trimmings to cut out leaves or other shapes to decorate the top of the pie; dampen and attach. Glaze the top of the pie with beaten egg or milk, make 1–2 slits in the top and put the pie on a baking sheet (cookie sheet).

6 Bake in a preheated oven at 220°C/425°F/Gas Mark 7 for 20 minutes then reduce the temperature to 180°C/350°F/Gas Mark 4 and cook for about 30 minutes until the pastry is a light golden brown. Serve hot or cold, sprinkled with sugar.

FREEZING

The pie can be frozen for up to 3 months.

SYLLABUB WITH BRANDY SNAPS

Centuries ago, syllabub was made by milking a cow directly into a bowl containing sherry or cider, and the resulting foam was skimmed off and served. Today we use cream, which makes a syllabub both thicker and richer.

STEP 1

STEP 2

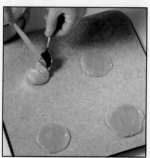

STEP 5

STEP 6

SERVES 4

finely grated rind of 1 lemon
2 tbsp lemon juice
60–90 g/2–3 oz/¹/₃– ¹/₂ cup caster
  (superfine) sugar
6 tbsp white wine
1–2 tbsp rum, brandy or sherry (optional)
300 ml/¹/₂ pint/1¹/₄ cups double (heavy)
  cream

BRANDY SNAPS:
60 g/2 oz/¹/₄ cup butter
60 g/2 oz/¹/₃ cup caster (superfine) sugar
2 tbsp golden (light corn) syrup
60 g/2 oz/¹/₂ cup plain (all-purpose) flour
¹/₂ tsp ground ginger
finely grated rind of ¹/₂ lemon

TO DECORATE:
fine strips of lemon rind, blanched
sprigs of mint

1 Put the lemon rind and juice into a bowl, add the sugar and wine and mix well. Leave to stand for at least 30 minutes, preferably 2–3 hours.

2 Add the rum, brandy or sherry, if using. Pour in the cream and whisk with a balloon whisk or electric mixer until it stands in soft peaks.

3 Divide between 4 tall glasses, decorate with strips of lemon rind and mint sprigs and chill for 3–4 hours.

4 To make the brandy snaps, line 2–3 large baking sheets (cookie sheets) with baking parchment. Gently heat the butter, sugar and syrup until melted, then remove from the heat and stir in the flour, ginger and lemon rind.

5 Drop 4–6 teaspoons of the mixture, spaced well apart, onto each baking sheet (cookie sheet). Cook in a preheated oven at 180°C/350°F/Gas Mark 4 for 7–8 minutes until golden brown and firm.

6 Quickly remove from the baking sheets (cookie sheets) using a palette knife (spatula) and immediately roll around a greased wooden spoon handle or greased cream horn tins (molds). Leave to cool on a wire rack. Remove from the handles or tins (molds) and store in an airtight container until required.

7 Serve the syllabub with the brandy snaps.

SUMMER PUDDINGS

A wonderful mixture of summer fruits encased in slices of white bread which soak up all the deep red, flavoursome juices. Make in individual pots for an impressive dessert.

STEP 2

STEP 4

STEP 5

STEP 7

SERVES 6

vegetable oil or butter for greasing
6–8 thin slices white bread
175 g/6 oz/³/₄ cup caster (superfine) sugar
300 ml/¹/₂ pint/1¹/₄ cups water
250 g/8 oz strawberries
500 g/1 lb raspberries
175 g/6 oz black- and/or redcurrants
175 g/6 oz blackberries or loganberries
sprigs of fresh mint to decorate
pouring cream to serve

1 Grease six 150 ml/¹/₄ pint/²/₃ cup moulds or cups, or a 1 litre/2 pint/ 4¹/₂ cup pudding basin (mold), with butter or oil.

2 Cut the crusts off the bread and line the moulds or basin (mold) with the bread, cutting it so it fits snugly.

3 Place the sugar in a saucepan with the water and heat gently, stirring frequently until dissolved, then bring to the boil and boil for 2 minutes.

4 Reserve 6 large strawberries for decoration. Add half the raspberries and the rest of the fruits to the syrup, cutting the strawberries in half if large, and simmer gently for a few

minutes until beginning to soften but still retaining their shape.

5 Spoon the fruits and a certain amount of the liquid into the bread-lined moulds or cups and cover with more slices of bread. Spoon a little more of the juice around the sides of the moulds or cups so the bread is well soaked, if necessary. Cover with a saucer and a heavy weight, leave to cool, then chill thoroughly, preferably overnight.

6 Purée the remaining raspberries in a food processor or blender, or press through a non-metallic sieve (strainer). Add enough of the liquid from the fruits to give a coating consistency.

7 Turn onto serving plates and spoon the raspberry sauce over. Decorate with the mint sprigs and reserved strawberries and serve with cream.

SOFT FRUITS

When soft fruits are out of season, replace them with about 750 g/1¹/₂ lb frozen mixed soft fruits. There is no need to cook them; simply thaw before use and use only half the quantity of sugar syrup.

CLASSIC HOME COOKING

ACCOMPANIMENTS FOR SOUPS

Scones

The recipe for crusty scones given with Thick Onion Soup (see page 8) can be varied widely. First of all replace the flour with 250 g/8 oz/2 cups self-raising flour and then add one of the following to the dry ingredients :

2 tbsp freshly chopped mixed herbs or one individual herb; 60 g/2 oz chopped walnuts, pecan nuts, cashew nuts or almonds; 45 g/1½ oz pumpkin or sunflower seeds (roughly chopped if preferred); 60 g/2 oz crisply fried and crumbled bacon.

Melba toast

This is a traditional accompaniment to soups, pâtés, potted meat, salads, etc and is simple to make but needs constant attention to prevent it from over-browning.

Cut the crusts off as many slices of bread as required – brown, white, granary, mixed grain, etc. Toast each side of the bread, then, using a sharp serrated knife, quickly slit the slice horizontally in half and scrape off any soggy crumbs. Put the slices, cut side up, under a moderate grill and cook until browned and the edges curl up – watch out as it burns easily. Serve warm, wrapped in a napkin, or store in an airtight container.

In writing a book on classic cooking, it has been very difficult to select a small range of recipes without omitting so many others which would fit in just as well and are equally worthy of a place in this book. So I have chosen to cover as wide a variety as possible, giving many new twists to old favourites.

Classic cooking covers many of the recipes that have been passed down from generation to generation and family to family to give us many of the well loved dishes widely used today. Many of them are not the most elaborate or complicated recipes to prepare, but are based on good, wholesome, everyday ingredients that are as widely available today as they always have been.

These recipes are used not only by families but also by top chefs and restaurants – they may well be given special additions to make them particular specialities, but they are still based on the original classic dishes. These famous and delicious recipes include several soups, main courses such as Boiled Beef and Carrots with Dumplings (see page 36), Shepherd's Pie (see page 40), Steak and Kidney Pudding (see page 43), and desserts such as Bread and Butter Pudding (see page 68), to name just a few. They use many of the simple cooking methods such as boiling, braising, roasting, etc.

It may seem from the recipes given in this book that all classic home desserts tend to be high in calories, but that does not have to be the case: there are many low calorie dishes too, but those featured do give a good selection of the real classics. You can cut down on calories by choosing to serve them with natural yogurt or low-fat fromage frais instead of the usual cream or custard. All the desserts can be varied to use a variety of spices, flavourings or fruits available at different times of the year: wonderful soft fruits in the summer, as with Summer Puddings (see page 74) or dried fruits such as prunes, apricots, pears, etc in the winter months.

INGREDIENTS

It is essential to select with care the ingredients you intend to use in your dish, and to make sure they are in tip-top condition and very fresh. When shopping, pick out the required ingredients with care, whether shopping in a supermarket or in a smaller independent grocer's, greengrocer's or butcher's shop. If you can spare the time, it is well worth shopping around. If you need advice, it is best to find a small specialist shop, for the shop assistants will be more familiar with their produce, which is particularly helpful when buying fish, meat, poultry and game. Greengrocers have excellent stocks of local produce and if you look for fruit and vegetables that are in season you'll find that prices are low while the food is of the highest quality. The availability of frozen, canned and imported fruit and vegetables means that we can enjoy all kinds of foods at all times of the year, but homegrown seasonal produce still can't be beaten for flavour and quality. What could be better than the first, fresh young peas of summer, or the crisp, flavoursome apples that appear at the beginning of autumn.

Fish

Fish is always popular and features in many classic dishes. Take care when buying fish; always make sure it is really fresh, check the 'use by' date on prepacked fish and, if you buy fish fresh to freeze yourself, make sure it has not previously been frozen. Fish is very perishable, but provided it is handled with care, kept chilled after purchase and used quickly, there is nothing better. Nowadays, whole salmon are very reasonably priced, and are no longer the luxury they used to be; but they still make a very elegant and spectacular centrepiece to a buffet or special meal.

To serve salmon hot, follow the method for Glazed Salmon (see page 24), but increase the cooking time to 10 minutes per 500 g/1 lb. When cooked, remove the fish carefully from the fish kettle and drain off all the liquid. Place the salmon on a serving dish and carefully strip off the skin. Serve with wedges of lemon and a hollandaise sauce (see Herrings in Oatmeal, page 22).

If you don't have a large fish kettle you can sometimes hire them from a fishmonger or from the wet fish counter of a large supermarket. Alternatively, the fish can be cooked in a large saucepan or preserving pan. Simply heat the water and other ingredients until just boiling, then hold the fish upright in two or three strips of folded foil and carefully lower it into the pan, curving it as you go. The fish will retain this shape and look very attractive when glazed. It is, however, not quite so easy to serve when cooked in this shape.

Shellfish

It is essential that all shellfish must be in prime condition, transported home as quickly as possible and, if fresh, stored in the refrigerator and used within 24 hours. Avoid shellfish that looks stale or has a strong, sour or unpleasant odour which will be quite apparent and different from the usual 'fishy' smell. Mussels need special attention; any that are open should be tapped sharply – if they don't close quickly they must be discarded, for they are dead and therefore poisonous. Mussels will open up during cooking, and any that remain closed should also be discarded.

Frozen shellfish is widely available and probably more frequently used. Again, take home quickly and store in the freezer if not to be used at once. Thaw out what is required either for a few hours at room temperature or overnight in the refrigerator. Once thawed, they should be well drained and used quickly. Do not let them hang around for a further 24 hours before use.

When it comes to freezing cooked dishes using fish or shellfish, they can be frozen for 1–2 months, provided the dish has been properly cooked, even if the main ingredient has been frozen once before. If the ingredients are just added to the dish at the end of cooking, as prawns (shrimp) may be, do not freeze it.

SALAD DRESSINGS
Whether served as a starter, a main dish, or as an accompaniment, salads are always enhanced by a dressing or mayonnaise of some kind, so here is a selection.

Classic mayonnaise
Once made, mayonnaise will keep in an airtight container in the refrigerator for 8–10 days.

2 egg yolks (at room temperature)
1/2 tsp mustard powder
juice of 1 lemon
300 ml/1/2 pint/1 1/4 cups light olive oil or other salad oil
1–2 tbsp white wine vinegar
good pinch of caster sugar
salt and pepper

Beat the egg yolks, mustard and 1 tsp lemon juice until smooth. Gradually whisk in half the oil, drop by drop, until the mixture thickens. Whisk in the remaining lemon juice and then gradually add the rest of the oil, a little faster than before, until thick and totally emulsified. Add vinegar, seasoning and sugar to taste.

Variations
Add the grated rind of 1 lemon or 1 orange; 2–4 crushed garlic cloves; 2 tbsp chopped fresh mixed herbs; or 1–2 tsp curry powder.

Cooked salad dressing

A delicious alternative to mayonnaise, both to add to salads or serve as an accompaniment.

1½ tbsp plain flour
1½ tsp caster (superfine) sugar
1 tsp mustard powder
6 tbsp milk
30 g/1 oz/2 tbsp butter or
    margarine
1 egg, beaten
3–4 tbsp wine or tarragon
    vinegar
4 tbsp sunflower or olive oil
salt and white pepper

1. Mix together the flour, sugar, mustard and salt and pepper to taste in a small saucepan and gradually stir in the milk. Bring slowly to the boil, stirring, and simmer for about 1 minute.

2. Remove from the heat and cool slightly then beat in the butter, followed by the egg. Return to the heat and cook to just below boiling, stirring all the time. Do not allow to boil.

3. Remove from the heat and gradually beat in the vinegar to taste, followed by the oil. Adjust the seasonings, cover and allow to cool.

4. Store in an airtight container in the refrigerator for 5–6 days. Shake well before use.

Poultry

All types of poultry can be bought fresh, chilled or frozen. Fresh birds should be stored in the refrigerator between purchase and cooking, with the giblets removed, if there are any, as soon as possible. Fresh birds can be stored in the refrigerator for up to 48 hours. Cover loosely so the bird can 'breathe', and keep on a rimmed plate at the bottom of the refrigerator so the juices can't drip on to other foods and contaminate them. Treat chilled birds in the same way, but frozen birds should be given the suggested time for thawing, whether this is done immediately after purchase or after further storage in the freezer. All frozen birds come with both thawing and roasting instructions. Thaw in the refrigerator and, once again, put on a plate to catch any juices. Make sure the bird, whatever type, is cooked as soon as possible after thawing.

All poultry must be thoroughly cooked to avoid the risk of food poisoning. To test if a bird is cooked, pierce the thickest part of the thigh with a skewer – the juices should run clear. Never put stuffing into the large cavity of a bird, as it may not reach a temperature high enough to kill any harmful bacteria. Stuff the smaller cavity at the neck end instead, and cook any remaining stuffing separately.

Meat

Most meat is bought fresh and prepackaged from a supermarket, often complete with cooking instructions and hints on storage and preparation. Once bought, large pieces of meat can be kept for two or three days before cooking (check the 'use by' date), but minced (ground) meat, offal, etc. must be cooked within 24 hours.

When buying from an independent butcher, hints on preparation and cooking methods will be given by the assistants if required, and they will suggest which types of meat need long slow cooking and which can be roasted or grilled (broiled).

Fresh meat should have a firm texture and not too much gristle or fat, although a certain amount of fat is needed to give flavour and keep the meat moist. If you want to reduce the fat content of a dish, it is better to skim it off the top before serving. Unpack any tightly wrapped meat, cover loosely so it can 'breathe', and store on a rimmed plate at the bottom of the refrigerator so any blood can't drip on to other foods.

When buying frozen meat, it is essential to thaw it slowly and completely, especially when it is to be roasted. It is possible to roast from frozen but it is rather tricky to ensure complete cooking and tenderness. Minced (ground) meat and chops can be cooked from frozen with care, but to my mind it is better to thaw all meat before cooking. Again meat that has been frozen raw can be frozen as a cooked dish, if thoroughly cooked, for up to two months.

Vegetables

Fresh vegetables are essential to successful cooking. If in a good condition, they will keep in the refrigerator or a cool place for 2–3 days, but for the best flavour and nutritional content, they should be used as soon as possible.

Never store vegetables in an enclosed polythene bag, they will 'sweat' and quickly deteriorate. It is best to take them out of the bag and store in a net or paper bag which allows them to 'breathe' and thus prolongs their life. If they have to stay in polythene, make several large holes in the bag to allow the air to circulate. Root vegetables will keep longer than green ones, and green vegetables and salads will last longer if kept in the salad drawer at the bottom of the refrigerator.

Game

Game covers a wide variety of animals, from feathered game and water fowl to venison and hare. All game is subject to strict laws on shooting seasons, so is only available fresh at certain times of the year, usually in the autumn and winter. Grouse is the first to become available – from 12th August – while the final dates for game are in February.

There are now many specialist game shops country wide and these and many of the larger supermarkets sell a limited amount of frozen game all year round.

All birds should be hung to improve the flavour of the game, help tenderize it and give the characteristic taste, but the weather conditions determine the length of hanging required. Usually 7–10 days is sufficient for pheasants and partridges while others need less time; water fowl for instance need only 1–3 days.

All game is very short of fat so needs extra fat or liquid to add moisture during cooking. Quarters of citrus fruit or onion added to the cavity help add moisture as well as flavour. Take care not to overcook game as it will become tough and dry. If you want to roast a bird, it is advisable to buy a young one; mature birds should be cooked slowly and gently to ensure tenderness. When roasting, slices of bacon laid over the breast help protect the meat and add flavour, and also make a good accompaniment when serving the birds. If preferred, remove the bacon for the last five minutes of cooking, lightly dust the breasts with flour and return to the oven to brown. If the bird is misshapen, however, it is better to leave the bacon in place.

Accompaniments for game

Roasted game birds are traditionally served with these accompaniments.

Fried breadcrumbs

45 g/1½ oz/3 tbsp butter or margarine
1–2 tablespoons vegetable oil
90 g/3 oz/1½ cups fresh breadcrumbs

Melt the butter or margarine and oil in a frying pan (skillet). When the fat is hot, add the breadcrumbs and cook, stirring constantly, until golden brown. Drain on paper towels and serve.

Bread sauce

300 ml/½ pint/1¼ cups milk
2 tbsp finely chopped onion
15 g/½ oz/1 tbsp butter
4 cloves
90 g/3 oz/1½ cups fresh breadcrumbs

Put the milk, onion, butter and cloves in a saucepan and heat gently until the butter melts. Add the breadcrumbs and cook, stirring, until the sauce thickens.

French dressing

150 ml/¼ pint/²⁄₃ cup olive oil
  or half olive and half sunflower
  or other oil
2 tbsp vinegar (wine, cider, tarragon, etc.)
1 garlic clove, crushed (optional)
½ tsp English mustard
¼ tsp Dijon mustard
2–3 tsp lemon juice
1 tsp caster (superfine) sugar
salt and pepper

Place all the ingredients in a screw-top jar and shake well until totally blended and emulsified. Store the jar in a cool place and shake well before use. This dressing will keep for 2–3 weeks.

Variations

Add the grated rind of 1 lemon or ½ orange; 2 tbsp chopped fresh mixed herbs; 4 tbsp chopped fresh chives; 1–2 tsp curry powder; or ½ can anchovy fillets, well drained and finely pounded.

INDEX